A LIFETIME OF

LOVE

& OTHER POEMS

VOLUME TWO

DON MIRABEL

A LIFETIME OF
LOVE
& OTHER POEMS

VOLUME TWO

Order this book online at www.trafford.com
or email orders@trafford.com

Most Trafford titles are also available at major online book retailers.

Printed in the United States of America.

ISBN: 978-1-4669-6278-1 (sc)
ISBN: 978-1-4669-6277-4 (e)

Trafford rev. 10/29/2012

www.trafford.com

North America & international
toll-free: 1 888 232 4444 (USA & Canada)
phone: 250 383 6864 ♦ fax: 812 355 4082

TO TRUE LOVERS EVERYWHERE: IF WE WERE

THE WORLD, IT WOULD BE THE PARADISE

TO WHICH WE ALL ASPIRE.

LOVE

Should I compare you to the rarest jewel?
It would be unkind to you. We cannot measure
love by the sparkle of a stone, cruel
its quality to blind to human treasure.
A jewel is only what we see in it
and he who loves it, simply, has love to burn.
No jewel enriched the proud woman who wore it
nor ever offered her love in return.

But value resides in you and you are rare:
there is warmth in your comfort; a sweet voice replies.
We have a world of private wealth to share
whose sparkle touches our hearts before our eyes.
If I compared the rarest jewel to you,
men might reappraise the treasures they pursue.

August. 1954

Don Mirabel

Is my love different from all other loves?
Do kings caress less fervently than I
and bring a regal bearing to love's moods?
Are idols humble, quick to laugh or cry
or does their audience crowd their private rooms?
Do rich men place a value on their love
or priceless to the poor because it's all they've got?
I know that I am different when moved
by love: I seem to be what I am not
or, better said, I am what I seem not
to be. And so, if Pilate's timeless query
is unanswered yet, I venture, "Love,"
unless other loves are unlike mine; then I
am proud to love as no man loved before!

February, 1957

I have become too much a part of you.
Our lives are sweet in what we share, sweeter twice
than each could live alone; yet, twice bitter too
when my torments are source for sacrifice.
Remain one bit apart, oppose my quick
response to the blackest side and all that's sad,
Angrily tell me my head ought well be thick
or little things will succeed to drive me mad.
Laugh, if laughter pains; treat me as a boy,
then kiss me fervidly; shame me if you will
'though others do not hear the sound of love
counterpoint your words. If all that gives me joy
is bound with me in gloom, then gloomier still
am I. Treat me thus—but do it all with love.

March, 1957

Don Mirabel

We pick out of the world what pleases us
and that is beauty and is as it should be:
a ruling purely of the heart and thus
one with which no other can disagree.
When pride turns choice to judgment and vanity
boldly guards it, then beauty is a public thing
subjected to standard and loved impersonally
for what compliment to the lover it may bring.

Let us not seek approval from the crowd
of what we choose or love at once, for we,
as perfect lovers chosen, may be proud
that what our hearts select reflects us perfectly.
   When standards rule even the very least,
   we mistrust ourselves and beauty becomes the beast.

November, 1958

I am not brave nor strong nor ideally made
in form or face. I have no talent for wealth;
my hands fumble and cannot grip the grade.
I haven't even the comfort of flawless health.
But these are physical things and surely beyond
the power of my birth; so, I may place
the blame outside myself and thus respond
to all who fling their better fortune in my face.

Yet, how explain the failure of the inner man?
I might more often be calm and not carry on;
be less concerned about a disrupted plan;
enjoy what's left rather than deplore what's gone.
    But I am loved and in my lover find
    redemption of my frailty of frame and mind.

January, 1959

The Mountainclimber

He summons all reserve of youth for one high goal.
Once sapped and gone it will not flow anew
and he will never come this way again.
Yet, there is knowledge gained, intimate as the soul
of life, upon that painful path leading to
the height that holds him high above all men.
But now achieved, there seems nothing else to know;
no greater heights to conquer lie ahead
and there is only one lonely way to go;
then, no longer leading, to reminisce instead.

So, too, with poets and all of us who strive
to extract from life what our talents will exalt.
However small or large, we all will live
one height once, save in my love which will know no halt.

April, 1959

Love is not an island eroded by the surging flood
of time. It does not break off by bits which float
into an ebbing past nor is it a bud
that never bursts, endlessly remote
from the moment of decline; but love, if true,
is proof against the withered pleasures that die
along the way and refuge from the slew
of sudden wounds that mere living will apply.

Lovers, whose love is only from fortune hewn,
are lovers self-contained but those whose hearts
adjust to luckless times and stay in tune
to love gain the sole reward that life imparts.
    If love will change with every change in life,
    then lovers are never truly man and wife.

November, 1959

This poem contains a slight revision of the sonnet
that appears in Volume One.

My world was narrow; no horizons reached out
to the ends of Earth nor beyond an outstretched arm
and myopic eye. There was little I cared about,
thinking little worlds were subject to little harm.
But, within the confines of my limited life,
all things small assumed such huge, preponderant size:
I had simply changed the content of my strife
and had not even the comfort of being wise.

When now I brood on little faults and fall prey
to the pattern of tiny, self-centered minds
that chase minor hours into a wasted day,
I act on the responsibility I find
in loving you. When my world is narrow now
I focus on you--a wider world to allow.

November, 1961

My heart has hungered to be heard, my mind is mute.
My eyes mirror my heart but my lips are lead.
Love leaps through its silent gate though words seem dead
and in the living is my love the more acute.
Yet, when love makes no speech, so too are fears unspoken
and shame and sorrow, anxiety and hope.
In the self-made dark of our wordless love we grope,
'though in the sharing are our burdens broken.

Still, it is the irony of love that holds my tongue.
I seek to spare you from my faults, preserve romantic
purity and so, true to myself, my poems fail.
My love runs deep though heroically unsung
and would choose a solemn stillness to pedantic
parody of feeling too bright for mere words to pale.

January, 1962

In condescension to our love, we chain
the precious hours of our finite life
to a mirrored mimicry of joy and pain,
'til patterns yield to age's painful strife.
We close our eyes upon the moment come
and wake when measured minutes so declare;
and all the vital time between, in sum,
is substance gone before, both foul and fair.

What, then, of love in routine manner nursed?
Do we drain dry the flavor of a game,
never achieve the ardor of the first
encounter, fail more because we seek the same?
  If lovers fail, then love is misconstrued:
  repetition is time regained and love renewed.

May, 1962

The following poem is a modified sonnet in that each line consists of four iambs instead of five.

My love is a towering redwood tree
menaced solely by Earth's mortal grief;
yet, despite an imposing solidity,
it sorrows at the loss of the smallest leaf.
My love is a star astride the dark sky.
a burst of bright eternity;
but time and space seem each dawn to die
as Sun assumes its ascendancy.
My love is a rainbow coloring life,
arching above all joy and pain,
prism'd by a lovely, loving wife;
yet, before the rainbow there must be rain.
   My love is pure in feeling and giving;
   Its imperfections are inherent in living.

July, 1962

Don Mirabel

Although we are lovers, we are mortals, too,
and like those less in love, we have the same
poor words that speak our joy or convey our shame
or yield a meaning of emotion far from true.
Our love is so calm a sea that should one rare
pebble break its surface its ripples are a storm
churning the still waters turgid and warm;
and a tiny tempest becomes more than lovers can bear.

Let us not fail to know that our love lives
also in anger and lips that merge may pry
apart with no love lost, though unhappily.
Judge the strength of love by the anguish that moment gives
and ponder the sole answer to this: "How can I
hurt you without more deeply hurting me?"

July/August, 1962

We bind our actions to laws or to our rules,
save love, which, true to lovers alone, thrives
beyond the standards of wise men or of fools
and is the blessed burden of their lives.
If, in the judging eyes of civil men,
the means I choose to live defy their law,
or I do not conform to reason, then,
in my own defense, may I earnestly implore:
"I am a lover first and all else last.
Measure me, please, by the depth and strength of love,
for I do not fit into the molds you cast
and cold rules are not what I am enamored of.
And I am loved no matter what I seem;
so love remains my truth, though to others a dream."

April, 1963

'Though culture and commercial art
by standard should be miles apart,
our commerce finds it culturally smart
to capture all our expressions of the heart.
If I felt impelled to write of love today,
would a publisher read *what* I have to say
or rather look for the special way
in which I tied my love to Valentine's day?
And, if he did, would he tell me I'm too late
but have really less than a year to wait
to feel this way again and then restate
my chosen words for Valentine's Day—they're simply great?

Is my love on a level with a child in school?
Warm on holidays, on others cool?
If today I conform to this "golden rule,"
Must I say, "I love you"—April fool?

April1, 1965

Swift streams flow daily toward the swelling sea
of words, the record of my life, treasures
sunken beneath the surface of shallow thoughts.
Speaking slick messages and mirroring me,
each endeavor deepens the buried pleasures
as ephemeral phrases sail to finite ports.

My poems are ripples of refreshing drops
and, like some pure perfume, stay fresh though spare.
Those treasures raised, those enduring moments rare
release the values that commercial talent stops.
How fragile all the thousands of words I write
that sap my mind struggling to rise above,
if every now and then I fail to ignite
the glow, the glory of a wordless love.

May, 1970

Don Mirabel

In the beginning there was love and little else.
Far away a world was drying out, nearby
the sleeping seeds of fortune burst their shells
but love was deaf of ear and blind of eye.
Time was unreal and we were lovers in a dream.
In our communion the elusive goals of life;
no wants and hopes to gnaw, no sins to redeem:
we floated free and pure as man and wife.
Then, protective hours eroded one by one;
the jealous world kept chipping at our dream;
blind eye forced open, we were not alone
and effortless energy bent to strenuous scheme.
  In the beginning, there are love and youth;
  until the end, they remain enduring truth.

October, 1971

Why is life a matter of time, a thread drawn through
infinite adjectives,
many things at once, and different things to different men?
Why celebrate the inevitable, the conservative
rhythm that catches and claws us again and again?
Love is the antidote of time
and age ought to be a matter of love.
Birthdays should not be a numerical climb
but the herald of another year of love.
And so I do not recognize your age today;
there are no numbers I am enamored of,
for you are never touched by time in any way
when I count only the years of our timeless love.

May, 1972

When the hours of our lives
are but the minutes of time;
when stairways are mountains
we cannot climb;
when our eyes blur the words
that used to be clear;
when our ears often question
the sounds they should hear;
when youth dances around us
as our memories smile;
when the tastes we once relished
have turned into bile;
when our bed frames a kiss
and a pleasant, "Good night";
when sad news of another
gives new meaning to fright:
then I'll know who I am
and the "why" of my life—
all those burdens I'll bear
because you are my wife!

October, 1972

Would I let this day go by
without a word to tell you why?
In spite of all the minor woes
of missed vacations
and last year's clothes;
Of a home in need of a coat of paint,
of machines that fail or at best are faint;
Of pressure rising to record height,
of the printed page going out of sight;
Of filial barbs biting away,
of bills I simply cannot pay.
I still love to laugh and childishly prance
and take you in my arms to dance.
All life's woes I can rise above,
sustained and warmed by the strength of your love.

February 14, 1975

Don Mirabel

There are so many ways to measure years:
as blocks that build enduring monuments
or the bricks that ultimately weigh us down,
as a balance sheet of joy, ennui and tears
or mere time from baby talk to sapience.
Some greet another year with an oath or frown.
But I prefer to hail it differently:
another chance to reach an aging goal,
and less of time to waste diffidently—
the weight of years belittles failure's role.
Yet, another year has meaning and only matters
because life's most important fact stays true:
you see, all hopes, all dreams, everything shatters
if this were not another year with you!

May, 1980

The many words it takes to say so little;
the many years to live but never enough
to reach much further than the mere middle
of all we planned to do. Sometimes, we scuff
only the surface and leave the rest undone.
Perhaps, whatever level we attain
is less than love and more the proper one,
excused by a lifetime of poetic rain.
I have no worlds to conquer, no fame to win;
ambition lies withered like winter's rose.
Yet, I have gained the top and the right to grin,
for I have achieved love such as no one knows.

October, 1980

I am no breed of macho lover
who deems love a conquest under cover.
I am no peacock-strutting dandy
who thinks of love as sugar candy.
I am a silent, sensitive man
who loves with all the strength he can.
I live for the moments that we share;
I live in that I truly care.
It is never a question of yours or mine.
I am not a one-day Valentine.
For the hundred qualities my heart attracts,
I find not one my mind attacks.

February 14, 1901

Collectors—the admiration we bestow on them!
What diligence and discipline adheres
to coins and stamps and even comic books,
but it is not the same for the collector of years.
To youth we are the grim reminder of a day to come;
to our peers a puzzle: which one
will be the first to fall? From those preceding us,
a woeful nod: futility attends the setting sun.
At fifty, not withstanding foods and fads,
aerobic dancing and cosmetic creams,
we have either fulfilled the promise of our youth
or live in the debris of our dreams.
Is fifty a time to ponder where we've all gone wrong?
Do we now see errors for which we must atone?
Or is it an age that suddenly scrambles our minds,
obscuring even the blessing that we are not alone?

O, why fear fifty? Those are not mere memories!
We *have* loved and laughed and we *have* won
and that same love will sustain us
for all our years until the journey's done!
So, to fifty, we say: our love defeats you!
All else are minor thorns along the way.
It matters not how anyone else treats you:
as I loved you then, so do I love you today!

May, 1981

Our love has come a long, long way,
through sunshine and through rain;
we've flown on wings of fun and laughter,
and we've been pierced by arrows of pain.
We've given the world a bit of ourselves
and now we watch a lengthening line.
Our hearts are bound and firmly fastened
in life's enduring and precious design.
Our years are many and yet are measured
not by wealth nor by accomplished ends,
but by the warmth, the love, the faith
of true and trusted lifelong friends.
   Twenty-eight years as husband and wife
   are all the meaning I need of life.

October, 1981

Everything changes:
Time sees to that;
Life rearranges:
cover gray with a hat.
Our girls have girls:
we're once removed;
you have diamonds and pearls,
but what have I proved?
I swim, you knit:
my, our lives are deep;
you stand, I sit,
but both of us sleep.
Ah, age you ruin a Valentine!
Is this to be my ode again;
to tell that lifelong gal o' mine
that all we can do is remember when?
No, you never did demand perfection,
and you'll always have my undying affection.

February 14, 1981

We are all runners in the marathon of time;
each mile a year never to be run again.
So slow at first, we assail the arduous climb,
and now, so swift, on the other side of the mountain.
We finish at different times but no one wins.
We gain our victories along the way
and hope that they will supersede our sins
in legacy left to runners of another day.
If, after all, our race has been worthwhile
despite little to show in jewels and treasures;
if still I run, wondering what it gains me,
it is having you to run with that lets me smile,
knowing that you are the source of all my pleasures
and that your love-throughout my life- sustains me.

May, 1982

Although I change, to you I stay the same:
from the boy of yore, fair-haired and knighted.
For fortune, no demand, for failure, no blame,
and no remorse for amenities slighted.
'Though not, you make me worthy of such regard
and I condemn myself for what I lack.
To live the image is surpassingly hard:
I wake each morning to press the self-attack.
Yet, it is all the essence of your love
and, if I do seem young, I have you to thank.
If I can get on with life, it's because I'm
still learning from you how to rise above
society's whirlpools in which others sank.
Love conquers change and soothes the sting of time.

October, 1982

Don Mirabel

Mirrors, break! Memory, be gone! One year more
now burdens all the rest. It is the straw
of pain that pierces through a pleasant past
to remind that all things young can never last.
Stop measuring endless time by the savage result
of years that trap us like some insidious cult,
while tiresome routines steer us through the day
as the dreams and values of youth fall by the way.
Each new year must be the start of time to come,
our lives no longer a mere statistical sum
from birth to death—a biologic entity
in the annals of man. Don't let the year bring pity
for what is gone and never again can be,
so long as I have you and you have me!

May, 1983

O, the ironic glory of another year:
thirty now garnered, a wealth of days and nights,
a generation of precious sounds and sights;
such treasures stored, what do we have to fear?
Only this: the more to add, the less to share.
As we bend, what matters the weight of gold we find?
A mountain of memories merely whelms the mind.
Time gives, yet time takes away: this we have to bear.
No, it's not the mass of years we celebrate;
it is not remembrance of a lengthening past
wherein all joys recede and never last,
nor the privilege of age that youth may tolerate.
   Only we two, bound in compassion and love,
   are what the gathering of years is made of.

October, 1983

Don Mirabel

The luster has left the pale blue eyes;
a buzzing fights the words I hear;
and heavy, heavy are the sighs
as age attacks each passing year.
The crown of gold upon my head
is not the captured sun of youth;
it's chemically induced instead,
to try to stretch, or hide, the truth.
In such condition this faded star,
less with vigor than with a whine,
begs you to let an old grandpa
be your broken-down Valentine.
But you've never judged me by my cover:
what lies beneath and not above
has always guided my lifelong lover
and set apart our special love.

February 14, 1984

Where is the girl I strolled with through village streets
whose pedestrian paintings are now memorable treasures?
The girl who caught my passion for Broadway's treats
and found something to share in all my pleasures?
Where is the girl who made summer a goal
I eagerly drove a hundred miles to attain?
The girl for whom fortune played second role
to my just "being there" in sunshine or rain?
Where is the girl of brown, shoulder-length hair,
of soft, smooth skin and big shining bright eyes?
The girl who swayed in my arms as we danced on air
and said love made success of even futile tries?
Where is the girl who gave youth a vibrant joy?
She's still here, thank God, and that's why I'm still a boy!

May, 1984

Don Mirabel

Relentless as the tumbling tide of time,
the world grows old, the past grows long and I'm
a stranger to the boy of twenty-three
who smiles two-dimensionally out at me.
Am I also stranger to the happy girl
who shares the pose—the oyster and its pearl?
Is change so insensitive to memory?
'Cause even that is doomed to die or flee.
That we shall not have come and gone and time bear
no imprint to show that we were ever here,
these meager words and profound thoughts I leave
in hope that they some permanence may bequeath.
　　Thirty-one—or sixty-one—years of shared joy and pain
　　shall not be lost, lamented, nor lived in vain.

October, 1984

Again, the fourteenth day
of the second month of another year.
In well-chosen words I'm expected to say
all the things about you I hold most dear.
It is no longer a boy
who, for the 33rd time
must confess a lover's joy
in a Valentine rhyme.
So, I will not speak of love
as though it were the passion
that days and nights are made of
but, rather, in maturer fashion.
Love is simply being there,
even at opposite ends of a room.
Love is accepting the 10th time you hear
about what or where or whom.
Love is the comfort
of a voice and a hand
that give their support
and say, "I understand."
Love is a dynasty;
it is each precious heir
who carries our legacy
when we're no longer there.
Love is not caring
about the growing book of age,
but quietly sharing
each remaining page.
Love is the two of us,
just you and I, kid:
'though gone is all the fuss
of youth, aren't you glad we did?

February 14, 1986

Another birthday but time's touch does not show it;
so softly and silent are the lines of age brushed.
How lucky I am—I want you always to know it—
from the moment my life by yours was forever touched.
Treasures have been lost and many are not to be had;
some faraway places are never to be seen.
Minor triumphs and times unbearably sad,
success elusive, disappointments keen.
But love transcends all dreams and desires;
makes the most of the least so long as there's health;
turns even the rain into the best of weather.
So, leave the lament to self-sorrowing criers.
For us, another birthday untouched by wealth
means we've just traveled another great year together!

May, 1986

When all the world wears a mantle of mist
and the sun seems never to break through,
the gloom becomes easier to resist
because I know that I'll come home to you.
When luck touches me, however rare,
and I ballet boldly with unbridled glee,
the fact that it is yours to share
gives it all the more meaning to me.
Marriages may lose their bond
and less may stick than sever;
so long as each of the other stays fond,
ours will surely go on forever.
It is indeed just you and me
as we go forward from thirty-three!

October, 1986

Don Mirabel

I cannot extol nor excuse the erosion of youth
nor otherwise welcome the weakness of age;
and although I am forced to confront the truth,
I prefer silence in life's loneliest stage.
So, expect no poems, no fervent words of passion:
I am bound to brood over all that might have been.
If perfection has always been my fashion,
then what rewards are there left now to win?
None that compare with those already won:
All of them find their source and strength in you.
If I am the cold earth, you are the warm sun:
I sense your presence in everything good I do.
　　Your love enriches my past and gives me hope
　　and for the onslaught of age, the will to cope.

May, 1993

Lovers are one in love but, in thought, are two.
What pleases me may not also please you.
There is no "absolute" in a thought or a word:
What enchants me, to you may seem absurd.
What is right today, tomorrow may be wrong,
For values change and "truths" do not last long.

So, do not see in dispute a lack of love.
Time and chance define what right and wrong will mean.
Luckily, we have the power to rise above,
So long as we allow love to intervene.
   On this Valentine's Day, I say to my wife:
   "Love is the only enduring truth in life!"

February 14, 2011

FOR CYNTHIA ON TURNING EIGHTY

How far we've come from children on our block!
The friends we've made; the memories we've shared.
Myopic and wild, I saw life as a timeless clock
and failed to appreciate the girl who cared.
But love slowly forged an unbreakable bond
that tamed the boy and forever inspired the man.
Love has been our purpose and carried us beyond
the mundane matters that disrupt a lover's plan.

When love comes first, other aspects of life must falter:
That love is truth was all we needed to know.
Against our love, ambition and fame did alter;
To live for love was the path we chose to go.
   You're the woman who taught me Love is the meaning of Life
   and blessed me by becoming my wonderful wife!

May 29, 2011

FIFTY-EIGHT YEARS

As our lives lengthen, our hopes and dreams descend;
as our bodies weaken, the less we comprehend;
as our world changes, we cling to pleasures past;
as the generations go, ours is now the last.
We simply relive our childhood when we pretend
our lives persist beyond our natural end.
The journey that begins when we are born,
at end is not a fate to resent or mourn.
Enamored of ourselves, we miss the pivotal point:
it is knowledge, not man, that we must anoint.
To save the species, we must sow the seeds
to grow the progress the next generation needs.
　So, what have we, with our long lives, given?
　We've delivered true love to the loveless world we live in!

October 17, 2011

Don Mirabel

As I grow older, my thoughts grow muddled and meager.
I sense my being preparing for the story's end.
My spirit fails and my heart beats less eager
and I am far less useful than I intend.

But you, my love, still lean longingly on me
and instill the strength I need to carry on.
You are my will to live and will always be
the lifeline of your moody paragon.

Love has been the antidote to all the pains
and irritants of age. It defines life
and, when all else departs, true love remains,
the adherent, the oneness of man and wife.
    I need no reminder, no special day:
    Our love lives in everything we do and say.

February 14, 2012

On the tide of time we sail into the unknown
unable to hold the helm and foil our fate.
A ship mercilessly tossing and windblown
as we give the world away to a faster gait.
'Though I deplore the sights I'll never see,
the technology that surely will break through,
how meaningless all these would seem to me
if I could not enjoy them all with you.

Another year will now go swiftly by
in an ever-changing world no longer ours.
We are the relics of poignant pleasures past.
Yet, this is no time for tears 'cause you and I,
although we count not years or days but hours,
share fervent love that will forever last.

May 29, 2012

Don Mirabel

FIFTY-NINE YEARS

For fifty-nine years, in fifty-nine ways, I've tried
to depict the art of love in poetic style.
I began with the start of love in hesitant stride
and probed every part of love for a long, long, while.
And now, at eighty-two, what more may I
assess of love? Without you, I'd be lost.
What life has blended can not be parted, say I:
one from the other can not be torn or tossed!
We must resist the hardships of our age,
detach ourselves from others' stresses and strains,
avoid the problems that we can not assuage,
be strong and make light of all life's petty pains.
   One last assessment I can impart of love:
   we shall forever be the heart of love!

October 17, 2012

OTHER LOVE POEMS

FOR MY CHILDREN &GRANDCHILDREN:

BONNIE, SUSAN, EVAN
MICHELLE, JENNIFER, ASHLEY
BETH, STACY, MICHAEL
EASTON, BRANDON

BONNIE

TO BONNIE, AT ONE YEAR OLD

How much less it means to you,
my little girl,
than it means to us.
We are not as innocent of time
and we are not as innocent of thought.
So, how or why shall I advise
from my painful knowledge
one so young, so pure?
Yet, what of importance
can I tell you
that you don't already know?
You know more surely of love
than we who are able to express it
and often choose to withhold it.
When your daddy feels two tiny palms
pressed against his face
or little arms folded snug around his neck,
indeed he learns of love from you.
Nothing is of more importance
at this or any age
than your capacity to love.
Let me leave advice to its proper time.
There is only one youth
and now, my child, it is yours.

November 13, 1955

TO BONNIE AT TWO

Mommy and I cannot remember when we were two.
We just don't understand how the world really looks to you
and, so, you wonder why we act the way we do.

Well, Bonnie, although you won't really know until you've traveled
the same number of years and the same path as we,
let me try to tell you why the hand that hugs also spanks:
the spark of spirit that suddenly ignites at 6 AM
and meets a carefree day, all little talk and play,
is far above the spirit that meets a routine day,
that buys the food and pays the rent and cleans the house,
or toils away its daily time unrewardingly.
Our levels, unfortunately, are apt not to touch at many points.
But when they do—oh, when they *do*, the hand that spanks
is then the hand that hugs and we absorb all of you:
the clever things you say, the precious things you do.
Love spills out upon you and ourselves
and we are like children, too.
When that is what you do to us, my little girl,
we hug so hard that we hurt the hand that spanks in haste.

November 13, 1956

TO OUR BIG GIRL OF THREE

We love what reflects us, what pleases us,
what is possessed by us. Yet, the more concerned
with ourselves, the more we demand all these together
before we give our love; and the harder fully
it is to love. Then, love is all taken
and not at all given. What we don't understand
angers us, who doesn't understand us irritates,
what is opposed to our understanding
makes us fret because, once again, we would take more
than we are prepared to give. A big girl of three
very rarely—at any one same time—
reflects us, pleases us, is possessed by us.
Nor does our mind entirely understand hers
nor often grant the validity of her understanding.
Needless for us to say,
the three-year-old mind can hardly fathom ours.
And so, we love and fret, love displeased or angered
yet love. Perhaps, there could be more of love
but, then, you'd have to be less a big girl of three.
I guess we've both a lot to learn.

November 13, 1957

S is for Six
and for the Start of Spring,
for a season of Smiles
and every Sweet thing.
S is for Seeking
to See, to be Smart,
for Skill and for Study
as School plays its part.
S is for Singing
and for Standing on Stage,
the Sound of music
at a Singular age.
S is for Sister
who Strives to attain
the Standard you Set
and, in all things, do the Same.
S, too, is for Sadness
and Sorrow and Strife;
may all three Stay far
from a Superlative life.
S is for Sweetheart—
a Source of pride Shall you be
that always will Swell
in Mommy and Me.

November 13, 1960

S even swift years in
E xiting parade,
V anishing childhood,
E merging young maid.
N ow and forever

Y our first act is played.
E ducation must guide you
A nd one lesson it lends is
R espect for your parents and
S ister and friends.

O pen your heart, full of
L ove endowed and make
D addy and Mommy exceedingly proud.

November 13, 1961

Time is swift; time is slow;
tomorrow's come, yesterdays go;
yet, at lightning speed or at a crawl,
today is the shortest time of all.
Yesterdays are made of years,
tomorrows made of hours;
but in the seconds of today,
buds blossom into flowers .
With each today, the flowers change,
the buds of yesterday seem strange;
tomorrow's plant seems hardly near,
then, suddenly—today—it's here.
For each tomorrow you gather in
a yesterday ages Mommy and me;
Your tree of life branches firmly up
as ours bends into memory.
Remember, Bonnie, 'though now you are eight,
it isn't very long to wait
before you reach the same today
that Daddy once thought was so far away.
So, think of us as you run life's race,
for it's our paths that you retrace.

November 13, 1962

Bonnie, think of life as one long play:
some years are scenes, some end the acts,
but minor or major, in its own special way,
each year affects the previous facts.
Your early scenes were swiftly played:
I recall the infant whose cheek pressed mine
and then in Act Two emerged a young maid;
behold her now: our Fair Lady of Nine!
Another curtain descends on the past.
At nine, a girl enters a bright new phase;
so, change the scenery, increase the cast:
more "world" will intrude on the part she plays.
'Though life is a play and the world a stage,
and all of us actors performing our part,
remember, the real things at any age
are those that are "acted" from the heart.

November 13, 1963

Don Mirabel

O, what an uncertain age is ten!
So eager to say, "Hello" to older ways,
but reluctant to say, "Good-bye" to childhood days
and never quite sure of "how" or "where" or "when."
Ten is a threshold, a thin edge of time:
as you step over, you're one step further away
from dependence on parents and what you do and say
are all your own on life's uphill climb.
Ten is a magnet with opposite poles:
one pulls faster than it seems you can go,
the other draws you back to make time go slow,
with you at the center of opposite goals.
Ten is an age both wide-eyed and wild;
ten is an age that laughs more than it cries;
ten is an age too young to be wise,
but also too wise to be always a child.

November 13, 1964

Is this really the eleventh time
we seek the words for a birthday rhyme?
How simple it seemed when you were one
and all of life was play and fun,
but each time more difficult to express
an easy road to happiness.
Childhood leaves you, year by year
and our best advice is not always clear.
Should we describe the world of adult complaining
and proclaim that childhood days are waning?
Must we say, "Don't hold on, it won't do any good,
extend your horizon to womanhood?"
You are still a child, if only to us
and so, we will only caution you, thus:
Do not assume attitudes of adult aspect,
for adults will see only a child's disrespect.
Listen and learn and, in silence, mature,
and then, when you speak, you will no doubt be sure.
Never disdain the capacity for laughter,
so easy for a child and more difficult ever after.
Waste no time on the faults of others and yourself:
life's greatest issues are not all in books high on a shelf.
Always be a young lady for what lies ahead
and always remember the things we have said.

November 13, 1965

Don Mirabel

Bonnie, if we could only see ahead,
how much better we would judge the present.
The past is little help: its days are dead,
although its memories grow mostly pleasant.
We then could see the problems of the current day
grow small compared to what our future life must hold,
like the baby who struggles to grasp its toes today,
two years from now will mock a similar sight to behold.
We are the prisoners of current events
that we can't evaluate until they're past.
The elusive talent called "common sense"
is really luck that has simply managed to last.
He, to whom luck has given power or place,
will presume to judge like some qualified scholar—
as the millionaire will scoff with phony grace
the value a poor man places on a dollar.
'Though reality is what happens to us today,
It's significance is a matter of degree.
"Conserve your efforts for coming years," I say:
I know, for twelve of age once happened to me!

November 13, 1966

The clustered petals, sheltered as they form,
now pry apart to blink at sun and wind and storm.
The doe, on sturdy legs, holds still as sound
identifies the peril all around.
The threshold is crossed, the testing ground of age
has come: it's time to be alone on stage.
Like the emerging rose or yearling doe,
it is not just by passing time you grow:
age is far less the mathematics of years
than it is what one sees and what one hears.
The world is wider now, stretching beauty thin,
right will often lose, venality often win.
Sort the sights and sounds on paths that you pursue
And never pine that the world is so unlike you.

November 13, 1972

How wistful *we* are, looking back on age nineteen.
If given the chance, how solidly would we stand
upon those sparkling shores of gold and green
and contemplate the conquests close at hand?
Knowing now that nothing in life is absolute:
To be right is to adjust; to love is to accept.
To do your best is to be resolute.
To win is to ape; to please is to be adept.
To overreach your goal is to compromise.
To have compassion is merely to say it.
To seize success is to see with another's eyes:
The game of life is all in how you play it!
A time in retrospect so clearly major;
A time so clouded to the ultimate teen-ager!

November 13, 1973

Ah, Twenty! Time's puzzling paradox:
a bridge and barrier both,
an age that's free to fly but loathe
to snap the safety locks.
How unprepared we meet this age,
the product of our past.
By longing for the warmth to last,
we reinforce the cage.
Yet, ripped by restlessness, we lash
even what we love the most.
With uncertain bent, we boast
an adult right to doubt, to clash.
Still, if not at twenty, when?
A stumbling start
by a soft and vulnerable heart
that may never be the same again.
Ah, Twenty, ill-treated when first we accost you!
We scorn, we withdraw,
we run away, sometimes we score,
but we covet you most when we've lost you!

November 13, 1974

Don Mirabel

Because the mind sees further than the eye
and stretches out much farther than the hand,
desire seeks goals we can not satisfy
and raises doubts we can not understand.
Life, in the end, is merely compromise,
for we can never know what might have been.
Beyond wherever we are another goal lies
and what we want may be what we never win.
Our dreams are often only time's dread ally
to drain our youth and, yet, if dream you must,
then follow it! Go, see! Even say good-bye
and force your bristling fears to succumb to trust.
Better to love us less now, as liberator,
than, in the debris of dreams, to fault us later.

November 13, 1975

Twenty-one transparent pages glisten in my eyes,
like a book of memories bound by a bridge of years:
Did I waltz, babe in arms, to soothe away the tears?
Did we walk, hand-in-hand, to the smiles of passers-by?
Did the striving school girl seek her daddy's aid?
Did strings gently plucked bring music to my ears?
Did we stumble through those trying teen-age years?
Did suddenly a little girl become a grown-up maid?
Now, another page propels us on the path
that time has paved. We take our parents' place
as they took theirs, with neither protest nor wrath,
for we have had the pleasure of the race.
Bonnie, let the world you happily enter now as wife
include a walk back, at times, along the bridge of life.

November 13, 1976

SUSAN

Compare with all the pleasures of the world
my baby's dimpled smile.
Compare with all the treasures you can hold
the hug of a laughing child.
No wonder of the world is half the sight
of baby one-year old;
a peeking, pointing, pouting babe, the delight
is better felt than told.
May your joy continue through the years ahead;
may all good things reward you
for those moments full of loving cheer you spread,
and may life show its kindness toward you.

January 10, 1959

What is a little girl of two?
Three feet of dainty gestures
in the air; three gallons of tiny tears;
twenty-seven pounds of love and hugs;
of stubborn wants and tender tugs.
What more is our little girl of two?
A day of dimples in fashion-vesture;
a night of fever and of fears;
a trumpeteer for equal rights;
a storm of sisterly slaps and fights;
but always a source of sympathy
for an unhappy Bonnie or Mommy or me.

January 10, 1960

Growing up is as simple
as one-two-three
and it shouldn't seem new
to your Mommy and me.
We've watched one little girl
pass this way before—
the first time's an experience,
the second time, it's war!
Big sister rebels
at the little one's attendance
since Susan has declared
her independence:
not always to follow
but also to lead
and four little rooms
resound with the need.
Tempers and tantrums
and "don't love anymore"
if Mommy or Daddy
should enter the war.
But her love rebounds
surprisingly fast
for Susan means love,
too deep not to last.
Her kisses and smiles,
her warmth and her sweetness
forecast a future
of lovely completeness.

January 10, 1961

One full year more and now she is four.
Time, in its flight, turns sound and sight
from an infant's cries to pert replies,
from a helpless form to a 3 ½-foot storm,
but does not alter the traits that exalt her:
her willing smile whose dimples beguile,
her eager hug so strong and snug,
her dainty demeanor, endearing to all who have seen her,
the beauty that glows on her skin, surpassed by the beauty
shining within,
but, of all, quite way above, the fathomless depths of a
measureless love!

January 10, 1962

Five is such a funny little number,
Made of two straight lines and one that's plump,
like a doll-cuddling kid curled in slumber
or a jack-in-the-box that's ready to jump.
Five seems almost as funny as four,
a little bit taller and heavier, perhaps,
but not as grown-up as a year or two more,
with the same tiny teeth, maybe one or two gaps.
Five is much smaller than the gallons of tears
that follow the miles of stubborn streaks,
and flow faster when Daddy's threats arouse fears
but always dry with a smile on deep-dimpled cheeks.
Five seems to flourish on the barest of food;
just like the birds, she can dine on a crumb,
but, unlike the birds, when it suits her mood,
Susan's dessert is a sweet-tasting thumb.
Five is all these and so very much more:
favorite dress, favored hat, "best" shoes and glove,
lipstick and perfume and jewelry galore,
a mind quick to answer and—always—a heart full of love!

January 10, 1963

Don Mirabel

How wonderful it is
to see time play tricks
when it turns a child of five
into a young lady of six.
Her gestures are dainty,
she walks with a swirl,
she loves everything frilly
and enjoys being a girl,
Her make-up is applied
with the utmost of care
and she'll spend hours a day
just brushing her hair.
She always admires
what the mirror reflects,
yet, we know from within
flows the charm she projects.
Still, our fair lady
has much of the child,
from smilingly sweet
to stubbornly wild.
But one quality reigns,
whether child or young miss:
the most tender love
in every genuine kiss.

January 10, 1964

S usan is seven, an
U nbelievable age!
S o swiftly time turns
A nother year's page.
N ow pictures and poems

I n their places we fix
S o that we may remember our

S usan at six.
E ven though the fleet years
V ary her form and her face, her
E ssential sweetness and love time can
N ever ever erase.

January 10, 1965

Don Mirabel

Is every girl approaching eight
inclined to label good things great,
unhappy to have her opinions wait,
and likely to start her homework late?
Does every girl on the threshold of eight
have an older sister to emulate
and a younger brother to tolerate
or, at times, at both to become irate?
Is every young lady at the age of eight
so full of feelings compassionate,
so kindly and quick to commiserate
that her parents' woes evaporate?
Does every miss as she turns eight
seek only causes to celebrate
and find in things the qualities that elate,
lending them her light by which to radiate?
Is it, of the girl of eight,
the sweet and universal trait
to innocently captivate
by her readiness to accommodate?
Do you know another girl of eight
so happy to congratulate,
not envious to imitate
and eager to participate?
Is it true of every girl of eight
that she delights in things that educate—
in each fact learned, the fuel to illuminate—
and, in every discovery, an awakened thrill to create?
No, it is a unique young lady of eight
who has the capacity to venerate,
is full of love and devoid of hate,
so that, even her father, can not exaggerate.

January 10, 1966

A year ago it surely felt great
to announce aloud, "I am eight!"
But now, it really feels fine
to boast and brag, "I am nine!"
A year will pass and probably then
I'll proudly proclaim, "I am ten!"

But the difference, my dear,
is not in the year
that separates one age from another.
It's the progress you've shown
and how you have grown
that impresses a father and mother.
If the world of a year ago still looks the same,
if you would still rather play the easy game,
if the sounds of the earth strike the same simple chord,
if yesterday's fun leaves you not one bit bored,
if a tear will not flow for anyone but yourself,
if no need to know leaves the books on the shelf,
there will be no real reason to celebrate,
for nine, then, is surely no different from eight!

January 10, 1967

Don Mirabel

Time is stopped when a camera clicks
and at two or four or even six,
we can chart in our pictures the growth of the charms
we could already spot in the babe in our arms.
Although time still seems so swiftly to pass,
the camera slows it while she's yet a wee lass;
but one day you focus your lens and then,
who stands before you but a big girl of ten!
You suddenly see what progress she's made,
for now life has traveled through its first decade.
Taller, yes, but so close to a maiden
that with the demands of the future we are all at once laden.
No more little girl: we must think in terms that are older
and help Susan's outlook grow bigger and bolder.
Yet, as our lens reflects her image sharp and clear,
there still shines the smile and the love that make her so dear.

January 10, 1968

What does it mean to be eleven?
Susan, I would try to move heaven
to be that age again!
"Now," I would say, "first decade's done,
taking with it childhood's fun."
Too soon? Perhaps, but then
ten childish years are quite enough:
the ten to follow need sterner stuff.
So, why should you delay?
Ask, and answer, "Who shall I be?
Let the world get ready for me!"
And why not start today?
Time will come and time will go
much faster than a child can grow;
fear not to seem too old.
Far worse it is at a later stage
to seem much younger than one's age:
the warmth of youth strikes cold.

What does it mean to be eleven?
Ah, Susan, between earth and heaven
a golden coin is tossed.
If it never comes back to the little girl's face,
it means a young lady has taken her place:
childhood is forever lost!

January 10, 1969

Don Mirabel

Twelve is such a tender threshold of time:
the lovely lingering lights of eleven
shadow the difficult adult climb
and turn gladly back to delight a boy of seven.
Oh, childhood, what a hard task
to give you up! You are all I know.
In you I am secure. Why ask
me now to let you go?
Still, a sign of age has touched.
The bloom of life begins.
Childhood, so innocently clutched,
must yield to worldlier games that no one wins.
Twelve is tender for what has passed;
twelve is tough for what lies ahead.
Susan, push out your horizon, be not last;
yet, of your childhood, cherish each precious thread!

January 10, 1970

Years are made of moments,
those tiny bits of time
we paste in precious albums
or record in rumpled rhyme.
And now the thirteenth moment
trembles in my hand,
for disbelief has scattered
all the child-like words I'd planned.
Can it be that the dimpled babe
I cradled in my arms
now radiates in every smile
an incipient woman's charms?
Is it true that other men
(much younger ones, of course)
now seek the pleasure of her company?
Will their gain be my loss?
But I have one advantage:
all those tiny bits of time,
those many precious moments
will always be only mine.
Yes, babe in arms or teen-age miss—
this I am certain of:
Susan Cara at any age
will endow her years with love.

January 10, 1971

Don Mirabel

Time touches with its gentle care
the face of thirteen, fine and fair:
the flash propelled by azure eyes
has a subtler cast, more worldly-wise.
The smile that excavates those cheeks,
'though ready still whenever she speaks,
now tells in its beguiling gleam
a whole lot more than it may seem.
The glow of nature, fresh as spring,
is often enhanced by cosmetic coloring.
Hair worn high and back a bit
reveals a young sophisticate.
The shrieks of joy, so spontaneously loosed,
endear her more for being genuinely produced.
Yet, of all the change that we have seen
upon the face now turned fourteen,
the abiding feature uncontained by skin
is the radiant charm that lives within.

January 10, 1972

The world is a magnet, attracted to age
and we its players who collide on its stage;
but they who bounce back, rather than bruise,
can successfully bend the world to their views.
Now that you've reached an age between
the formative years and the adult scene,
the pull of the magnet may cause you to stumble
but right yourself proudly, don't ever be humble.
Let your eyes serve your heart and with firmness of mind
go after your goals and, if you can, be kind.
Luck is a legend; success is a scheme
and legion the players deluded by dream.
No dreamer's a doer; so, don't begin,
for a dream becomes only what might have been.

January 10, 1973

It is not enough to be sixteen and sweet.
Time withers and humanity corrupts.
Search now the source, the soul of Susan; meet
life with a goal that survives when the world erupts.
Believe firmly in yourself; let no one shake you.
Rarely does confidence so abound in man
that most are not awed by the convictions of a few.
Grasp boldly all the moments of glory you can!
Perform, beguile, dissemble if you must,
except for those you love—with them be real!
Shield your motives most of all from those you trust:
the frailty of friends inflicts wounds that never heal.
Whatever your goals, alone or as a wife,
build toward them with steadfast love, the mortar of life.

January 10, 1974

"Free my hand," the artist softly but firmly beckons,
"I would enlarge the canvas to hold deeper hues
"that shape the years ahead. Brush out the seconds
"of time past: now a larger sweep I choose,
"to give the future the strength of spirit soaring
"on colorful paths independently proclaimed.
"No more the lines of a one-dimensional drawing:
"my mural will abound with bolder strokes unchained."

The future ties us with a thinner thread;
independence demands a separate stage.
Events once shared become just yours instead;
sidelined, we can but encourage or assuage.
Responsibility gains a singular thrust:
to seventeen, it is *we* who must adjust.

January 10, 1975

Don Mirabel

At eighteen the world is wider and harder to grasp;
a thousand swift steps on a myriad of paths;
fleeting faces that claim their moments and gasp;
confusion of time and place, of facts and fads.
The future flashes as the younger years fade;
real and imaginary melt into fuzzy view.
Now you must separate substance from charade
and sift through people and places and pretense, too.
The world is callous now and couldn't care less:
you cannot pet it to make it purr, nor tickle
to make it laugh nor win it with a caress;
it is not easily conquered, firm yet fickle.
It opens only to knowledge, effort and skill,
to strength of purpose and persistent will.

January 10, 1976

There is no simple time of life. No age
limited to primitive pleasures pure and free.
We're burdened by dynasties of pride and rage,
victims of the past and our higher mentality.
We are not the chosen inheritors of the earth
if woven into a web of unnatural rules
that chain and shape us from the time of birth,
obligate us to goals of self-pollinating schools.
At nineteen, avoid the analytic end,
laugh long and never stoop to answer why;
pity the malice of a conforming friend
and fear no freedom your heart may want to try.
Giving love is the only simple time of life
that drains from living all frustration and strife.

January 10, 1977

Don Mirabel

Graduation—is it the measure of our youth,
molded in a classroom, prepared, pre-shaped?
Perhaps, graduation is more like birth:
nourished but untouched. Some have finally escaped
to meet the world head-on. For others, however,
the world never leaves the classroom, safe secure
as a fetus in the womb. They will not sever
the cord, unless life insists, "Decide, be sure!"
What a world they miss who do not face it.
In the end, what have they been, if not
just another animal. We can't retrace it,
only regret what we never gave nor got.
Time now to put the minds of others to rest
and let your own discover what is best.

June, 1979

If I were not to write this poem for you,
what would I have wrought? Would time stand still?
Would you remain forever only thirty-two?
Pity, the world is not bound to my will.
My silence will not stay the surge of time,
and I must speak to the swiftness of the years:
there *is* wonder in bearing witness to their climb
but, increasingly, I see it through my tears.
Still, so long as these lines are read by those after me,
so long will Mom and I transcend the ages.
Then, as now, you will be young and thirty-three,
for time can never touch these birthday pages.
And if, each time, one truth leaps forth, indeed,
it is the love that weaves the words you read.

January 10, 1991

Don Mirabel

Parents are supposed to make all things better,
to comfort, to soothe, to explain;
But 'though we may strive to the very letter,
Sometimes we simply can not ease the pain.
The age that you've reached, we would gladly deny
and defend it with credence and purity,
even though, by protecting the innocent lie,
we could lose our social security.
Alter history, if you wish, but where does it end,
as truth is battered and worn?
You become many years younger than every friend,
And you had your children before you were born!
Simply accept it, like a 40-karat diamond or pearl,
and should that fail—just think: you'll always be our *little* girl!

January 10, 1998

We measure time by years—I wonder why:
Am I any different from the year before?
Would anyone suspect if I chose to lie?
I'm exactly the same, I'm still as poor.
I'm the picture of youth, just see what I wear;
my thinking is young, my demeanor's the same;
not one strand of gray in forever-blond hair.
What's one more birthday if deception's the name of the game?
So, pile on the years, I really couldn't care less.
I won't change just because Father Time wants me to:
I proclaim it now, "Eternal youth is my happiness!"
And, as how to grow older, I haven't a clue.
One other thing: how old can I actually be
if my father himself is only forty-three!

January 10, 2003

Don Mirabel

EVAN

What are the ways of a boy of two?
A typical day may enlighten you:

Dawn breaks at six to the music of "Ma,"
momentarily stilled as he drinks his "ba;"
then a half-savage rhythm splits the air
as the house suddenly vibrates to "yeah, yeah, yeah!"
Out of his crib and into his clothes—
to find him we follow our ears or our nose.
All things once so neat strewn all over the floor;
so, we change him and hustle him out of the door.
The world's his arena; he charges out like a knight.
Woe to him who is there, for he's ready to fight.
If one sister or the other is entertaining a friend,
the game they are playing abruptly will end.
Now the shrieking and crying in voices loud and clear,
"Mommy, will you pul-lease get him out of here!"
You rush to their aid to see what you can do.
but how do you punish a "monster" of two?
So you scold and you spank and firmly say, "No!"
but severity softens when he puts on his show.
He laughs and he runs and he argues his case
with expressions of mischief lighting his face.
Then Daddy decides to answer the call
and hopes to divert him with, "Let's play ball."
He runs for his bat and swings like a pro,
then blasts the ball and his Daddy's aglow.
Just look at his father: you'd think he struck gold,
his boy is an incomparable two-year-old.
He's so busy complimenting and flipping his lid,
he doesn't see "angel" using his bat on a kid!

And so the day ends in exhausted joy:
now you know all about our two-year-old boy.

September 12, 1964

Don Mirabel

The time has come to turn the page
from two years old to three of age,
but how can I write something sage
when he has us ready for a padded cage?
Look at him at three of age,
shining bright, as on a stage.
Can *he* be the cause of parental rage,
sometimes difficult to assuage?
We're told "the *real* boy" is the gauge
by which to measure Evan Jay.
By this standard then, I'll wage,
all other boys are *fakes* at three of age!

September 12, 1965

Well, we "let him" and now he is four,
but before he advances one year more,
we must slow his phenomenal high-speed drive
or we'll need psychiatrists before he is five.
He's Batman and Robin rolled into one
and he pounds and he zams as if it were fun,
but his friends aren't Riddlers or Jokers, you see
and they don't appreciate his Batman spree.
Then, in his magnanimous, four-year-old way,
to Jimmie or Michael or Chris he might say,
"Now, you be Batman and you be Robin..."
then, what happens? The Riddler or Joker must win!
So, off to the doctor, this child he must see.
One look and Doc asks, "Is he on LSD?"
"Well, what can you do, Doc, you're medically wise?"
"In my professional judgment, tranquillize!"
"Ply him with pills at four years of age?"
"What would you prefer, an iron cage?"
At this point there's anything we're willing to try:
Tranquillizers it is; now he flies twice as high!
Yet, in spite of his mischief and sleepless nights,
in spite of his freshness and endless fights,
if we appraise his behavior in all honesty,
we must admit that he simply has more energy than we.
His good points abound: how he loves, how he nuzzles,
and he's really a whiz at mastering his puzzles.
So--no matter what we have to say,
we wouldn't change him in any way!

September 12, 1966

Don Mirabel

And so he's passed the age of four.
If you ask, "How was he different from before?"
An answer isn't hard to find:
four was the year of the inquiring mind.
The "whys" and "wheres" leaped from his lips
like missiles from their battleships,
bombarding their target, lucky us—
until he learns the word, "ridiculous!"
Now that he's five, will it change anything?
Will we still often hear the doorbell ring,
only to have some playmate tell us:
"You know that Evan hit Marcellus!"
Will school now harness the energy
that strengthens him and weakens me?
Or will his presence forge his name
and the school will never be the same?
This is the beginning of a little man
who suddenly discovers that he very well can
perform with all his vigor and vim
those things his mother once did for him.
Five is a declaration of independence
(which may even extend to his school attendance).
Five is a sudden growing-up,
the threshold of youth, no longer a pup.
Five is the age of bat and ball,
of hikes and swimming—he's ten feet tall!
Yes, five is an age of genuine joy,
yet, he still remains our *little* boy!

September 12, 1967

When every moment explodes with sound
and endless energy bursts all around;
when a bicycle with rider high
zooms recklessly and swiftly by;
when a strong-armed hurler offers proof
by landing toys unerringly on the roof;
when a house is a speedway for matchbox cars
and the walls display their silent scars;
when a Tarzan shriek and a lightning dash
accompany the swimmer in his diving splash;
when the doorbell rings and one by one
we learn of something else he's done;
when all these things form a special mold,
you have a picture of Evan at six years old.

And, yet, there is more that ought be told
of the sensitive boy, as well as the bold:
the boy who reads and loves his books,
the boy who cares about how he looks,
the boy who writes and proudly displays
his masterpiece for just a bit of praise.
Yes, the boy whose energy cannot be capped
has a well of love unfathomed, untapped.

September 12, 1968

Nine is a four-letter word,
like ball and play,
like free as a bird,
like bike, riding swiftly away.
Nine is a song
in a husky throat,
a swim with a strong
and steady stroke.
Nine is a speed ride
aimed at the sun:
toboggan high, parachute wide,
it's a world full of fun.
The road of this world
is haphazardly strewn
with shoes and socks deftly hurled
in room after room.
Nine looks at food
as a killer of time;
so, all meals are half-chewed,
held by hands full of grime.
Yes, nine is a four-letter word,
like pals and, possibly, pets—
but the greatest ones he has ever heard
are the team at Shea, the fabulous Mets!

September 12, 1971

G et it together, son, time
R uns faster than you live.
A sk yourself how high you want to climb;
D on't expect more than you care to give.
U ncertainty is, at worst, a failing,
A t best a brief waste of years.
T arget your goal and set sailing;
I mbed it too deep to be touched by fears
O r doubts. Success is the sum
N ow of all the days to come.

June, 1979

Advice is an arrow without a bow, falling
far short of a target moving too fast. A dad
is a waning observer who again hears the calling
of the youth, the vigor, the dream and the chance he once had.
Now, I hold the arrow; God, where is the bow?
Having lived the past, I see the future too well.
How can I make eighteen understand what I know
or make it listen to what I have to tell?
Time is your competitor, luck is a fable.
Believe in yourself because confidence places
us higher than wisdom. A loser who learns is able
to win the world and command the future he faces.
    Decide what you want; let nothing deflect or delay:
    better to sweat the chase than to dream life away.

September 12, 1980

Is the world no more than a pile of dirty clothes,
a lament to perceived obesity?
Is it simply a mirror-image pose
Assumed too often and too easily?
Can the world be only a sportsman's paradise
Reluctantly interrupted by social demands?
Is it a lair of leisure that otherwise
needs no development of mind or hands?
What of the wars that rage on other soil?
Technologies that redirect our lives?
The inverted politics of greed and oil?
The liberql goals toward which no nation strives?
At twenty, the world's the oyster that hatches us—
until the noiseless net of time lost catches us!

September 12, 1982

Don Mirabel

There are no bends in the road of twenty-two,
no notions to deter the delight of the dream.
There are burdens it must avidly eschew
lest life's charm be less than it may seem.
For, twenty-two is but a moment lost
between young pleasure and adult principle.
If most favor the former at any cost,
for that brief moment, they are invincible.
Despite my wisdom of the world ahead.
I am not wise enough nor willful to fault
The pull of freedom that fails too soon. Or, instead
to phrase an insistent cry: "Gird for the assault!"
No matter what I say or what I do,
It was yesterday that *I* was twenty-two.

September 12, 1984

Twenty-three, yes, twenty-three:
what a marvelous age to be.
I can not stem a nostalgic surge,
as all the emotions of time converge.
If I derive from this one word of advice,
born of experience and somewhat wise,
since I have already paid the price,
it is, my son, organize!
Visions dissipate and ambition runs thin,
when unaligned with discipline.
They must be balanced, even to suggest,
that what you do, you indeed do best.
Time is no ally of youth, no friend,
nor knowingly wasted on a long-term plan
that is not lost until the very end:
when manipulated, maturity marks the man.
Think, especially as you see the grand
potential that broadens every business shore,
and you may yet hold the world in your hand
by the time you are twenty-four.

September 12, 1985

Don Mirabel

Another year attaches to the rest,
and it is I, not you, who wonder and wince.
You feel one rung higher toward being the best
and impatient with those you must convince.
Life faces only west to meet the sun:
you soar only where blue cloudless skies abound.
Who owns the shades of east is the negative one,
whose feet have surely never left the ground.
But life is a balance sheet where every gain
is diminished by unwelcome disappointment.
I simply can not deny that there is pain
nor neglect the frequent fly in the ointment.
You see sun, I anticipate rain, and yet,
the older we become, the closer we get.

September 12, 1986

Our son is now a quarter-century old
and a millennium ahead of us.
He sees challenge to be met forthright and bold;
we see it as a foe and perilous.
At twenty-five, he is where I had hoped to be,
and to higher goals by ambition driven.
The difference—only fools could fail to see—
while I have only dreamed, he has striven.
He mistakes my fears for resentful reins;
my indecision for a tearing-down.
He counters with boasting and flaunting gains,
generosity to others and painting the town.
   So, let the record be set: we proclaim it aloud—
   Evan, your mom and your dad are exceedingly proud!

September 12, 1987

Don Mirabel

Nature tries and, when she fails, she tries again,
one lucky combination sure to strike it right.
It seems she must produce ten thousand men
to give us one in whom we can delight.
At twenty-six your fame is far and wide;
(mine narrow and confined to family and friends)
unafraid to venture out (I instead might hide),
instinct serves a sharper means to worldly ends.
Now, the glory I had dreamed I glean from you:
I bask in the sunshine of my own son;
I am proud of almost everything you do
and through it all am even having fun.
I see you finishing what I could only begin,
and you will be what I once might have been.

September 12, 1988

Twenty-seven is truly a pivotal age,
poised between the upward climb and the rare crest
of success. In its way, it is a passionate page
of life and, in retrospect, a triumph or a test.
At twenty-seven, you are your own creation,
and no one can give you direction or advice.
You find your own path to every destination,
and rarely do you follow the same route twice.
For most, the luxury of twenty-seven
is self-contained, confined in a narrow sphere.
The age itself is their brief brush with heaven
but what they do only a few see or hear.
For you, Evan, the world is open wide
and a host of loving people are at your side.

September 12, 1989

Whatever your world may seem at twenty-eight;
no matter how much of it you mold or master;
you are never the complete captain of its fate,
and can not will it to move slower or faster.
'Though you call the music, the world may not dance to your tune.
Bestow a smile and it may return a frown.
What you will build, others may try to ruin,
but as long as you stay up, they will stay down.
You harm yourself to dissipate in hate
the energy that sets you ahead, and apart
from all who envy, slander and imitate.
They touch not your talent; don't let them touch your heart.
How much the world allows you of what you've planned
will depend upon how well you understand.

September 12, 1990

A decade ends but not the daring dream
to do, to become whatever you want to be,
to personalize the world, to hear and see
this fickle, malleable orb as it ought to seem.
Damn the crowded tracks of time, the future plan,
to which too many others conform and bend.
It is not in your interest to play the part, to pretend:
In every lifetime there should be one Peter Pan.
The trouble is an insistent world intrudes,
envious of those who live outside its rules,
trying to destroy the spirit that soars free.
But he who yields is soon the one who broods,
subjects desire to all the proper schools:
there, my son, lies the difference between you and me.

September 12, 1992

EVAN AT 40

Forty is a "Catch-22"---
So much accomplished; yet so much to do.

Don't get hung up on "The Way We Were,"
"High Anxiety" doesn't suit ya;
"Ride The High Country" on "Blazing Saddles"
And never turn your "Back to the Future."

There were "Days of Thunder" and "Body Heat"---
A "Raging Bull" found his "Place in the Sun;"
Then learned that mistakes can cause a fall
Even when you reign as "Top Gun."

Dreams will always "Die Hard"
If you live as an "Easy Rider;"
But one "Fatal Attraction" is all you need
For life to take a slider.

It may seem that "It's a Wonderful Life"
To squander wealth while savoring wine;
But a guy can go completely "Psycho"
Seeking "Deliverance" from "The Bride of Frankenstein."

Being a "Dad" is "The Natural " part
That every man wants to play;
It lends your life "A Touch of Class"
And gives meaning to your day.

So, look on yourself as "The Graduate,"
Ready to start fresh, young and new.
Avoid "Close Encounters of the Third Kind"
And don't let life depend only on "The Turn of the Screw!"

September 12, 2002

(Needless to say, Evan is a movie buff)

EVAN, AT FIFTY

For you, my son, how swift the race of time,
for me, one step closer to the finish line.
Words defy me to assemble an appropriate rhyme
as your journey presents an enigma to define.
I picture the boy with energy galore,
who kept sorrow within when his grandpa passed away,
later refused to build a cushion safely in store,
but insisted on only living for today.
We've watched you reach the heights in royal style;
we've seen you in the bitter depths of life,
impetuous, depressed and all the while,
saddled with a depraved, demeaning wife.
You've raised two sons of whom you're rightfully proud:
one with budding promise to be a titan of the stage;
the other a magnet for a female crowd
at an awesome and utterly early age.
Now, at fifty, the urge to start again,
body and mind rewound, rejuvenated.
This time, will you master a business regimen?
Will loyalty of those you trust not be fabricated?
A shining new horizon beckons you;
you've conquered the stigma of middle age.
Armored with a mature, yet youthful, purview,
it bodes a compelling and successful force you wage!

September 12, 2012

Don Mirabel

MICHELLE

Child of my child, how well you conquer time
when you hug me and I hold you and when we dance.
Swiftly, the years recede and once again I'm
The ecstatic father of the first circumstance.
What love and pride, what pleasure you endow!
From the moment you sparkled like a precious gem
behind a nursery's drab window pane 'til now,
you've been a special rose on a special stem.
'Though you may shun sleep to stay upon your toes.
'though you may be selective of what you eat,
these are no faults but simply your parents' woes
and, in our eyes, history prone to repeat.
Perhaps, a deeper feeling infuses this poem
for, after we've loved you, your parents take you home.

May 20, 1979

The road of life in two short years
has become a two-way street:
the sights she sees, the sounds she hears
are now carried on running feet.
"A bird, a plane, and Daddy's car,"
a "Tiny" doll and "table and chairs,"
a walk around the block so far,
and twice a terrible "boom" on the stairs.
Pictures and books and records, too,
"Tomorrow" spinning again and again
"Grandma, sing 'Adoraboo'"
and other songs from way back when.
But of all the wondrous sights and sounds
that suddenly seem new,
the one to which my heart so wildly bounds
is: "Grandpa, I love you!"

May 20, 1980

How can I put upon this page
the broad smile upon my face,
as my brain vibrates with words so sage,
so disarming, so full of grace?
The smile is broad because the words are not mine,
yet they are the most powerful poetry;
so, call me no plagiarist if I quote a line
first spoken by a little girl of three:
"Grandma, how many times must I tell you
the things I did today?"
With an impatient gesture performed so well you
are left with absolutely nothing to say.
Ah, what a precious age is three:
a playgym slide, with swings and bars,
a yellow-bird world called Sesame
and a rainbow world called Oz.
A red tricycle that soon will ride
mile after circular mile,
drawing forth her grandpa's pride
and her sister's dimpled smile.
But three is not all angel eyes,
and certainly not above
a wild display and angry cries
that only her grandma could love.
Yes, three is a puzzle, our little Miss,
but how well the pieces all fit;
just one long hug and a hello kiss
and we wouldn't change Michelle one bit!

May 20, 1981

Ah, the mystery when one is four:
is this Michelle who opens the door?
Her beauty radiates in the palest of light...
of course...we know her...she's Snow White!
Suddenly, she disappears inside;
well, grandpa's here, so it's time to hide.
Now in closets and corners I peek
to get my hug and kiss on the cheek.
Ah, here she is, grown so elegant and tall...
why, she must be Cinderella at the ball!
But who's that hiding just behind her?
She's Cinderella too...she's Jennifer!
Look! There's Scarecrow, Tin Man and Cowardly Lion!
And Wicked Witch is up there flyin'!
Just snap your fingers, Michelle, and they will go
way back over the colorful rainbow.
Enjoy this time, for when you're old like me,
you rarely are what you want to be.

May, 1982

M y, I can't believe she's already five!
I t seems but a moment's passed since that joyous drive,
C rowning a night of anticipation.
H ow vivid the memory, how warm the sensation!
E ager to welcome our daughter's daughter;
L o, the many things we had already bought her.
L ife now lets her reciprocate,
E xuding love to her *old* playmate.

I n her hand, a work of art,
S tuck and colored from the heart.

F orever enthralled by a story read,
I t eases the pain of going to bed.
V ividly recalling the words that delight her,
E ach day dawns just a little brighter.

May 20, 1983

Don Mirabel

Ah, my little magician,
how quickly you turn five into six,
making us all a little older
with your time-tampering tricks.
From the cradle to first grade
in no time, it seems;
less and less the child and more
the future answer to some boy's dreams.
You're a master of games
you play with grandpa,
and at mastering art forms
proudly "hung" by grandma.
Bigger words and numbers
show growth and grace,
and silly small talk
no longer has a place.
Yet, for all the wonder of Michelle,
there seems to persist a
sibling's impulse—sometimes—
to be mean to her sister.
But the magic continues
and those cantankerous urges
will surely disappear
as the young lady emerges.

May 20, 1984

Oh, what a trying age is seven,
especially when you're the oldest child:
everyone expects you to act like eleven;
it's enough to drive a little girl wild!
"You're the big sister," they always say;
"so set an example and you be strong."
That means that Jennifer should get her way,
even if what she does is wrong.
Well, just because I'm tall and thin,
my hair is stylish and layered up,
my permanent teeth are coming in,
that doesn't mean I'm all grown up!
But I will heed this silly advice,
if you promise to repeat it to Jennifer.
Let's see if she will act so nice
when Ashley is four and teases her!

May, 1985

Don Mirabel

The world widens a little more,
the stage grows somewhat broader;
life's a bit more complex than before,
with more demands and more disorder.
Nine is such an awkward age
that can set your head awhirl.
Is it the start of another stage
or still the world of a little girl?
Tall and slender, glowing and fair,
the changes seem so swift to me.
'Though nine is neither here nor there,
it carries more than a hint of what is yet to be.
Fashion leans toward teen-age fads,
And boys are curiosities.
The break begins from moms and dads;
now, it's one's peers that she must please.
Still, younger sisters, and cousins too,
ask for attention to be paid.
After all, they look up to you;
so, another role must be played.
No, it isn't easy to be nine,
But it's fun to play so many parts.
Enjoy each minute of this precious time,
for some day soon, you'll be breaking hearts.

May 20, 1987

Oh, the threshold of eleven:
just steps away from all that leads
from a child's simple needs
to a teen-ager's complex heaven.
Going are all the games and toys,
giving way to lyrics suggestively sung,
and full-length posters, decoratively hung,
of movies' and TV's most popular boys.
A piano played progressively better;
a dancer who sways and flips;
a head of curly hair swept back with clips;
and suddenly new significance to a sweater.
But one thing strikes most impressively—
of all the others it is far above:
the warm, sincere and growing love
she openly shows to Grandma and me.

May 20, 1989

Don Mirabel

Ah, twelve is such an awkward stage,
poised on the threshold of beckoning teen-age.
Nothing at twelve seems to go right,
as you struggle with feelings neither black nor white.
Are you all grown up or are you still a child?
You like the safety of home, yet hear the call of the wild.
Parents seem often opposed and intent to deter you;
why must they always question or demand: "Where were you?"
Your capacity to judge is greatly underrated
and school, unfortunately, must be tolerated.
Yet, through all the torture of growing up,
perseveres warmth and love, like a cuddly pup.
The desire to delight and successfully please:
there are no traits more endearing than these.
Twelve, too, will pass—time is the cure,
and Michelle will blossom as her qualities endure.

May 20, 1990

Who is Michelle? She changes so fast,
it's hard to know. We remember the child
with the wistful look and her leg in a cast;
but no matter how it hurt, she always smiled.
Who is Michelle? The little girl who made
the living room her stage, directing each part
that her sisters and cousins played.
But it's she who stole the show—and our heart.
Who is Michelle? The young lady who strives
to win a role with confidence and poise.
We suspect an intention to brighten *our* lives
or is it her motive to impress the boys?
Who is Michelle? She's a special thirteen
and win or lose, our reigning queen.

May 20, 1991

Sixteen years are like the yesterday of time,
touching us all but mostly transforming you:
The little girl's a woman, and now the climb
of life begins—'cause what you say and do
will matter more and what you are will mean
everything to a career or to a wife and mother.
Be sincere: sincerity won't trap you between
words and deeds or fuel the frenzy of another.
For now enjoy your moment in the bright sun
of youth. Savor this precious interlude,
which comes but once. Count yourself as Number One
(not one of many) and never let pressure intrude.
Sixteen is but life's brief and passing treat;
it is far more important to remain always sweet.

May 20, 1994

JENNIFER

Jennifer is one,
and one is a person
ready for fun:
like pulling down objects
that narrowly miss her,
or tearing up books
that belong to her sister.
One is a snuggler,
Her head on your shoulder;
one is a hugger,
who makes you eager to hold her.
One avoids sleep
like time that is wasted;
but food is her fuel,
so, everything is tasted.
One is a tugger,
who quickly informs you;
one is a lover,
with a smile that warms you.
One is a child
with an inquisitive mind;
Jennifer is one—
yes, one of a kind.

February 3, 1982

Two is twice as big and strong as one:
one walks, while two is always on the run.
One points with fingers on chubby hands,
two waves impatiently and makes demands.
One nibbles and distrusts her food,
but, to eat, two is always in the mood.
One may not nap, but always sleeps all right,
two would rather stay up all night.
One follows her sister closely, in awe,
two wants equality and wages war.
The change from one to two is plain;
for Mommy and Daddy it's quite a strain.
But for Grandma and Grandpa everything Jennifer does
is adorable and beautiful—the best that ever was!

February 3, 1983

J ust one minute, please!
E verything moves so fast!
N othing stays still—well, maybe, the trees—
N ow, another whole year has passed.
I see our granddaughter growing tall,
F air of feature, dainty, and free;
E ach forceful gesture—how well I recall—
R esolved to start each sentence with, "Me!"

I n the blink of an eye, the curls have gone:
S traight thick hair now frames her face;

T wo big blue eyes spilling tears upon
H er Mommy's shoulder—she won't take second place!
R adiant charm , as she swirls in her dresses,
E xudes from her smile and
E nvelopes you in her caresses.

February 3, 1984

Why can a girl of four be such a riddle?
Warm and loving, yet other times shy?
With Grandma and Grandpa stuck in the middle,
it's hard to understand why she would want to cry.
Then, she'll hug and kiss 'til our cheeks are wet
and tell us she loves us a hundred times.
Awash in her smile, lost in her laugh, we simply forget
the pout that out of nowhere suddenly climbs.
She's eager to please when she plays with her sister,
dressing their dolls in outfits galore;
but sometimes she feels the need to resist her,
when *her* ideas ought be considered a little bit more.
But woe to the one who dares scold Michelle:
Jennifer's the lawyer who argues her case,
the fighter who defends her sister's honor so well,
there's never a doubt who'll emerge in first place.
Reading and learning are things that can wait.
Perhaps, in a year or two she'll give them a whirl;
but now it's more important to investigate
all the frills and the facets of just being a girl.

February 3, 1985

Don Mirabel

How do you measure the size of a hug
that two little arms can form?
How do you measure the depth of a smile,
winsome, winning, and warm?
How do you paint perpetual motion
in an endless change of clothes?
How do you describe how beauty or charm
emerges, develops and grows?
How do you capture a beginner on skates,
gliding over the ice?
How do you tell of the sister in the middle,
alternately naughty and nice?
How do you show the desire to learn
that has suddenly come alive?
Well, all you need do to give it a name
is to call it Jennifer at five!

February 3, 1986

What can we say of Jennifer
as the camera clicks;
how can we properly picture her
at the age of six?
Eyes bright, giant peas in a pod,
smile, wide and winsome,
clothes fashionable and mod,
jewelry galore and then some.
A certain flourish, a certain flair
that embellishes the frill;
she whirls and twirls and floats on air:
femininity is her skill.
Her thoughts come quick, she speaks her mind
and tells it like it is.
There is no doubt that she's the kind
who will demand you call her Ms.
Independent in the light of day,
she can't be alone at night.
So what if she must have her way,
for time will only prove her right.
'Though Jennifer may seem to be
only a little girl of six,
it's really a miniature woman we see,
as time plays its timeless tricks.

February 3, 1987

Don Mirabel

Nine is such a troublesome age.
when everyone tells you what to be.
I'm not an actress on a stage,
all I want to be is me.
Why can't I be left alone
instead of being told what I must do?
I know, at nine, I'm not full-grown,
but can't *I* decide what, where and who?
Others my age may conform
and act as grown-ups expect.
Who is the genius who set the "norm"
that decides what is wrong and what correct?
Accept me for what I am today:
loving, caring and inquisitive.
What I feel is what I say
and, of what I say, I am positive.
One day, all things will fall into place;
I don't know where or when;
but I refuse to be pushed into a race,
and I will continue to be me until then.

February 3, 1990

Ten is both an ending and a beginning:
the start of a new decade.
Waiting ahead, the struggles and the winning,
and the teen-age plans to be made.
Ten is the start of so many things:
tenderness is just one;
when displayed, such satisfaction brings
that its warmth challenges the sun.
Ten is also the start of transforming the pup:
tension is bound to find you.
It is merely part of growing up,
as you leave the care-free years behind you.
Ten is an age that demands to be heard,
confounded by all of the changes.
Tenacious is not just a ten-dollar word,
but a protest when life rearranges.
Ten means saying good-bye to the past
and hello to the years ahead.
They all approach surprisingly fast—
so, listen to your heart but also your head.

February 3, 1991

Don Mirabel

ASHLEY

When Ashley is one,
what does she see?
Toys all around
and birds in a tree.
When Ashley is one
what does she do?
Claps hands, waves "Bye-bye,"
and "Oh, my goodness" too.
When Ashley is one,
who tends every plight?
Mommy and Daddy,
all through the night.
When Ashley is one,
who makes her laugh 'til she's hoarse?
Michelle and Jennifer,
her sisters, of course!
When Ashley is one,
who makes her eyes widen and flash?
As Grandpa hugs her and holds her,
she tries to take off his mustache.
Ashley, now that you are one,
whatever you see or you do,
the world is at its widest,
just waiting for you!

May 10, 1986

Don Mirabel

If I were a designer creating a doll,
where would I begin?
Hair straight and soft as golden silk,
curling under a button chin;
eyes big and blue and, oh, so gentle,
revealing light long lashes when they close;
lips prepared to pucker and kiss
beneath a tiny upturned nose.
Arms outstretched and eager to hug
or to nestle her head on your shoulder;
Even if you've had a pretty rough day,
everything brightens when you hold her.
Finger nails with ruby-red polish—
the feminine world has a beginner—
a body shaped as if ordained
to be a future contest winner.
And if she spoke, what would she say?
Not just a simple word or two,
but sentences and thoughts and many things,
and her favorite phrase, "I love you!"
Yes, if I were to design a charming doll,
wouldn't that one be perfect to hold?
Well, nature has beaten me to it:
She's called Ashley at two years old!

May 10, 1987

A little girl is growing up—
S wiftly, sweetly, sugar and spice.
H er smile shines brighter than a butter cup;
L ove drenches the lips that kiss you twice.
E very word is precisely spoken,
Y et not without an actress' flair.

I s this the portent of hearts to be broken?
S hall we say it now: "Young men beware!"

T omorrow should not be our concern today,
H old tight to these years that pass so soon;
R ight now, a little lady holds sway,
E njoy her fully, like a day in June—
E njoy her fully, they're playing Ashley's tune.

May 10, 1988

Don Mirabel

A little girl is growing up
   faster than one-two-three;
   sweet, yet saucy, soft yet stubborn
   and pretty as can be.
S hy at times, more likely coy,
   but a natural with her peers;
   if only her strong-mindedness
   would allay her night-time fears.
H er role as sister is not unique,
   but a thorn in the side of her mother:
   she seems to have mastered the mischievous knack
   of playing one sister against the other.
L ove glows in the twinkle of an eye,
   and in the charming ear-to-ear smile;
   then, the warmth of a kiss bestowed
   lingers for a long, long while.
E very word is precisely spoken,
   and many are strong and regal;
   often with emphatic gestures
   to make her edicts perfectly legal.
Y es, this is the Ashley of today,
   and we look forward to much much more;
   but we leave that to the years ahead—
   right now, she is only four.

May 10, 1989

A little girl—the littlest of three—
S tands tall and pretty as can be.
H ow grand it is to watch her grow,
L ovely and loving from head to toe.
E verything about her is appealing—
Y es, she imparts a special feeling.

I nto the pool with one bold leap,
S wimming in water that once was too deep.

F ashion, however, is more her flair,
I nterest in clothes and fixing her hair;
V ivacious, demanding, soft-spoken or loud—
E very grandma and grandpa would feel just as proud!

May 10, 1990

Don Mirabel

If I were to search the whole world through
to find a girl whose eyes are big and blue;
if I were to seek a wide sweet smile and blonde hair, too,
I know my search would end with you.
If I were to look for a girl who's good,
who does all the things a good girl should;
if I were to look as hard as I could,
I am sure it is clearly understood
who the girl would most certainly be,
as the clock of years steadily ticks:
none other than playful, laughing Ashley
at the tender, formative age of six.

May 10, 1991

BETH

Picture a dimpled smile
that seems to say,
"Smile with me,
I'll brighten you're day!"
Twinkling blue eyes
with a special gleam
that can turn a drab world
into a delightful dream.
Picture a sunset
suspended in air,
then settling softly
on each strand of hair
on a head snuggled securely
on her grandfather's shoulder,
as he dances delighted
that he can never grow older.
Picture a finger,
pointing with glee,
to tell you emphatically.
"That's for me!"
A mouth preciously puckered
and framed by her hand,
to chide you, but cheerfully,
if you don't understand;
then suddenly saying
a word that astounds you,
or miming your actions
until she completely confounds you.
Picture her curled in a crib, cuddling
her doll—her day is now done.
Picture all that and, yes,
you have a picture of our Beth at one!

February 5, 1983

Picture Beth at the age of two:
a liberal sprinkling of red in her hair;
determined eyes of twinkling blue
seem to say, "Guess what I'm going to do!"
A winning smile that commands all to share.
Picture Beth waiting for grandpa to show:
the door opens and, lo! she's in seventh heaven.
But even grandpa she doesn't want to know,
and everyone else can get up and go,
when she's locked in the arms of her uncle, Evan.
Picture Beth scattering toys in the den,
building a block house with windows and doors,
but never so creative as those times when
she attacks even herself with a ballpoint pen
or rearranges all the displays in the stores.
Picture Beth concerned about Ernie, Bert and Big Bird,
if they should have troubles on Sesame Street.
Listen! She just used an unusual word,
we hadn't known she had ever heard.
Yet, as smart as she is, she has no socks on her feet!
Picture Beth bathed and shining bright,
Ready for bed—if you dance with her, Sue,
but not without Dolly, whom she's clutching tight
and who will provide her with comfort throughout the night.
Now, you have a picture of Beth Lauren at two!

February 5, 1984

Picture a face that beams with delight
in the shimmering glow of the TV screen,
while we marvel at the charming sight
and that she understands what the characters mean.
Picture two hands that quickly assemble
the pieces of a cartoon puzzle, or draw
a gallery of pictures that resemble
the subjects they are intended for.
Picture her printing every alphabet letter,
or winding a band-aid around a blister,
or petting sick Stacy to make her feel better,
and sharing her crayons with her inquisitive sister.
Picture a mouth that is prone always to smile,
speaking softly or rising to a shout,
uttering incredible words all the while,
like, "Grandma, I'm just hanging out!"
Picture a mind that differentiates inches and feet,
absorbs Dr. Seuss from cover to cover,
understands the difference between messy and neat,
and knows how to make everyone her enchanted lover.
Picture a pert little form dressing herself,
matching her clothes with near perfection;
but also throwing a tantrum if the red-headed elf
can't call the plays or set the direction.
Now, assemble the pieces; put them together:
what do we have; what do we see?
Clear as a bell in sunny weather—
lo and behold, a picture of Beth Lauren at three!

February 5, 1985

I don't believe in birthdays,
no matter what the date.
How can you celebrate being four
when you seem to be six or eight?
Does a four-year-old use the words
you expect from children nine or ten?
Does any other child print these words
like a master of the pen?
Are the thoughts and ideas of adults
things a four-year-old would understand?
Do other children of the same age
serve as teacher's second hand?
How many four-year-olds watch TV shows
from beginning to the end
and, although they are meant for older eyes,
find them no problem to comprehend?
That's why birthdays from now on
will never be the same.
If I am a disbeliever,
four-year-old Beth is the one to blame!

February 5, 1986

Don Mirabel

It is not just a little girl
who outwardly grows.
All that makes her special
each year more strongly shows.
The precious traits
that time reveals
are in every embrace
that her grandpa feels.
When someone hurts,
Beth cares;
when a friend has less,
Beth shares.
When anyone needs help,
Beth lends a hand,
then, quite patiently
makes him or her understand.
When sister and brother fight,
Beth sends up doves,
and the world becomes a better place
because Beth genuinely loves.
These are the special traits
that contrive
to paint a picture of our Beth
at the age of five.

February 5, 1987

Beth is like a blossom whose petals
eagerly unfold to absorb the sun and rain.
Before the dark night settles,
there is growth she must attain.
The need to know, the will to learn—
horizons broaden every day.
With boundless energy to burn,
Knowledge brightly lights the way.
A world of words to master,
many of difficult sound and sense;
yet, she pursues them ever faster,
until pursuit incurs impatience.
Then, frustration forms a flow of tears
and irritable rejection.
But it's not inability she fears—
it's simply Beth's quest for perfection.
Still, sweetness and caring always prevail,
and popularity knows no limit.
Invitations come daily in the mail:
"Shine on my party; you're absence might dim it."
So, another year focuses in my lens,
and my camera proudly clicks.
I wonder what this year portends,
as I capture our Beth at six.

February 5, 1988

Don Mirabel

B is for beauty:
   we watched it begin;
   it grows year by year,
   radiating always from within.
B is for bright:
   she makes it quite plain
   that understanding and knowledge
   find a fertile field in her brain.
B is for big,
   as sister to sister:
   in reading or writing
   or even tending a blister.
B is for brother:
   whether a hawk or a dove,
   she shows him an abundance
   of brotherly love.
B is for Brownie,
   one of the Girl Scout rookies
   who, in her first year,
   sold the most cookies.
B is for best
   in whatever she does:
   she strives for the top
   and makes it uniquely hers
B is for Beth
   (if there is one) from heaven
   to charm her grandparents
   at every age, but now at seven.

February 5, 1989

How long I've struggled with this birthday poem,
failing to discover the words I need
to tell about a special girl
in simple terms that she can read.
Is "beautiful" enough to reflect her face?
Is "brilliant" enough to describe her mind?
Is "caring" enough to characterize her heart?
Aren't there better words that I can find?
She is the daughter every mother wants;
she is the sister siblings crave;
she is the grandchild who makes us proud;
she is the student about whom teachers rave.
Yet, she's so hard to capture in rhyme;
perhaps, there are several years to wait;
and so, I must settle for well-worn words.
After all, Beth is only eight!

February 5, 1990

Don Mirabel

What a lucky age is nine!
The world does not yet crowd you.
Each day dawns carefree and fine
and we all like what you say and do.
Enjoy this age—it comes but once.
Don't let impatience push the years.
You have now what everyone later hunts:
a simpler time with minor pains and tears.
Nine is an age when body and mind team up,
urging you to try, to discover, to do
whatever you wish, whatever you dream up.
It is the beginning of the unique you!
You are special; you are Spring's fresh breath;
at nine, there is indeed only one like Beth.

February 5, 1991

Sixteen, Sweet Sixteen:
And now you are in-between
the girl you are to grandma and me
and the woman you are soon to be.
School is still a breeze,
with mostly A's and just a few B's,
and only one subject that muddies
a report which otherwise shines—Social Studies.
Yet, in the big picture, its significance shatters
for *you* are the social study that matters.
Basketball, photography and visual art,
a sweet disposition and a boundless heart:
these are the qualities that society rewards—
if life is a symphony, your years are its chords.
So, develop your talents, go after your dream:
Disseminate your love and life will always be:
SWEET SIXTEEN!

February 5, 1998

Don Mirabel

FOR BETH, AT THIRTY

Ah, to be Thirty! What I would gladly give!
Using what I know now, I would know how to live.
But time and age can not—will not—ever wait,
And experience and luck temper our fate.

So, Beth, rely on your talent, your brain and your dream,
Discern what is genuine, not what something may seem.
Trust your heart and your mind, beware contrary advice,
For those who may envy can be artificially nice.

You have youth, you have beauty, and you shine with love;
You're to be desired—you're a cut above.
Be true to yourself, never doubt your goal or your will;
If truth should be imperiled, then never be still.
　　Beam with laughter and joy and always a smile
　　And life will be lovely and fully worthwhile!

February 5, 2012

STACY

One is to get ready
to steal the show:
Here's Stacy, unsteady
and she won't let go.
She clings to her Mom.
whom she can't do without;
so, with Stacy on her arm,
Mom carries one inside, one out.
There's always a big smile
lighting her face,
as she crawls mile after mile
all over the place.
Her sister's her joy
who makes her laugh;
but sister's book is her toy
she shares by tearing in half.
The sounds of a song
brighten her day,
but when she sings along,
the birds fly away.
She cuddles to grandpa
as he dances high off the ground,
and snuggles to grandma
if Mom's not around.
Her teething's a pain
that ruins her fun,
but Stacy makes it plain
that she's glad to be One.

January 9, 1985

Stacy is two
and it's time to review
everything new
now that Stacy is two.
For months she did balk,
then, rose on her feet
and decided to walk
...a bit like a stork.
Now she runs here and there,
even descends the stair;
her legs sometimes carry her
no one knows where!
Her crib has been shed;
she now sleeps in a bed,
and never has to be led
when she's Miss Sleepyhead.
Her bottle's gone, too;
only a cup will do,
just like you-know-who,
now that Stacy is two.
If one thing's amiss,
it's simply this:
Stacy just isn't sure
of whom she is.
What she will do and say
is but the replay
or a second display
of her sister's way.
Yet, parents, take heart,
it's really an art
to follow the start
of a teacher so smart.
And now there's another,
to whom *she's* the mother:
she can be her own person
to Mike-y, her brother.
Any story of Stace
must mention her embrace
and the bright sunny smile
that lights up her face.

January 9, 1986

Don Mirabel

S is the smile she's never without;
T is the toys her brother strews all about.
A is the arms that tightly press;
C is the charm of a loving caress.
Y is the year, big number three

A nd a pretty young girl who never says, "Me!"
T o share with her sister is important to her;

T o follow her, too, seems what she'd prefer.
H ide in her shadow? There's no fear of that.
R ead the signs right: she will wear her own hat!
E ach younger sister has this problem to face;
E xactly how many-under three-can tie their own lace!

January 9, 1987

Stacy is four
and one year more
delightful than before.
All sweetness and smiles
smoothing the miles
of childhood's trials.
The hugs and the kisses
that she never misses—
oh, what a lover this is!
With a big sister to imitate,
her own personality trait
doesn't mind a slight wait.
Then there's little brother to seize her
and constantly tease her,
but not overwhelm things that please her.
She loves going to school
and to parties with peers who'll
be sure to play by a gentle rule.
Yes, Stacy is four
and a life of love galore
is what the years have in store.

January 9, 1988

Don Mirabel

It's fun to be five
and watch the world come alive
with things you never saw
when you were only four.
Like going to school
and learning things that are new;
it's exciting and cool
to discover all you can do.
To make many a friend
and receive invitations they send;
to be popular and, all the while,
wear a warm and winning smile.
To learn how to read,
opening a new dimension;
a sister, Beth, is all you need
to make you pay attention.
Being five is such fun,
you don't even mind the one
upsetting note that can strike
in the form of your brother, Mike.
There is a time to enjoy—
like a treasure every one hunts—
the goal of every little girl and boy:
You are five only once!

January 9, 1989

S is for Stacy,
Sunny as can be,
Smiling and laughing,
a Sweetheart is She!
S is for Smart—
Suddenly it's known:
She hides in no Shadow,
She Stands on her own.
S is for Sister
Sandwiched between
a Soft touch ahead and, behind,
a hard Striking machine.
S is for School
and for Studying well;
for Seizing math concepts,
and learning how to spell.
S is for Special
and also for Skirts;
for Sincere Signs of love
and Squeezing 'til it hurts.
S is for Six,
an age that's a Start.
To make the road ahead Smooth,
continue to Speak from the heart.

January 9, 1990

Don Mirabel

S is the Start of So many words:
it's a Squiggly letter that's the Start of Snake.
But it also Stands for the Sounds of Birds,
and, yes, for Stacy, for goodness Sake!
S is for Sweet and also for Smart,
for eyes that Shine with every Smile,
for the Special beat of a Sympathetic heart,
and for Sobs and Simpers once in a while.
S is for School and for Skirts with patches,
for Seeking the Solution to every riddle,
but it Stands also for her brother's Scratches,
because Stacy, you See, is the Sister in the middle.
Now, S is for Seven, a Stand-out age:
Soon a young lady will Suddenly appear.
She will be at the center of the Stage—
ah, but that's a Song for another year!

January 9, 1991

S ixteen is such a wondrous year;
T ime is the magician:
A girl whose smile is sweet and sincere
C ontinues the tradition.
Y es, she is a young lady now

I n every sense of the word.
S he walks in beauty and shows us how

S weetness can be felt and heard.
I f we could see her being,
X rayed, and soul laid bare,
T ruly we would be seeing
E xcellence residing there.
E very parent's ideal indeed is she.
N ow and forever, lovingly.

January 9, 2000

MICHAEL

The fact that Michael is already one
both wonder and joy imparts;
but it's the portent of things to come
that strikes terror in our hearts.
His sisters' screams are sure to grow louder
as he interferes in every game,
and his mischievous grin is sure to grow prouder
as they hit him and heap him with blame.
Mommy will need four sets of eyes
to follow his rapid movements.
For disrupting the house, he will take the prize,
and don't expect any improvements.
Daddy will try to channel his vigor:
maybe sports, such as a ball and a bat,
but somebody's bump on the head is bound to get bigger,
and Mike's laugh will proclaim, "How about that!"
Yet, sometimes he acts shy and buries his face
and presses Mommy with all of his might;
but he's certainly not shy as he sets out on his race
to disrupt everything in sight.
Still, what's to worry, he's heaven-sent,
so, he's surely worth all the bother.
After all, he has ample precedent:
His uncle, Evan and, of course, his father.

July 10, 1986

Don Mirabel

Although Michael, at two, has doubled his age,
the increase in energy is impossible to gauge.
From out of his room comes a deafening clamor:
is he building or destroying with that little toy hammer?
Then, suddenly, a resounding crash and a boom,
but, not to worry, there goes Michael with the broom.
Now, onto his tricycle and out to the deck,
no feet on the pedal, yet, he whizzes like heck.
Then, up on the chair and onto the table:
you feel he would fly if he thought he were able.
He knows what he wants and is quite a resister;
if you want to confirm it, just ask either sister.
We tell him it's wrong if Stacy always cries,
but he makes it right by fluttering those big blue eyes.
With his mischievous grin and his foreign chatter,
he soon convinces you that nothing's the matter.
He's got rhythm and style and a dramatic flair;
he's a tumbler who yet finds time to care.
There's plenty of love, without hugs and kisses:
things that Beth and Stacy do are not things that *he* misses.
If two is an age of boundless pep and energy,
what should we expect when Michael is three?

July 10, 1987

M is for Michael and much, much more:
M is for motion—his feet hardly touch the floor;
M is for Mommy and all the mother love he can take;
M is also for "Mommy, I gotta make!"
M is for mischief by this little mister;
M is for making life miserable for his sister;
M is also for music and mimicking a song;
M is for the microphone that helps the medley along;
M is for merry and macho and marvelous;
M is for the Mirabel he got from us.
Put all the M's together and what do you see?
A pretty accurate picture of Michael at three!

July 10, 1988

Four is an age of big steps "four"ward:
of questions that show developing thoughts;
of going to camp, happy and stalwart;
of fearlessly trying all kinds of sports.
Four is an age of words spoken clearly;
of independence to do as he pleases;
but also the age of loving dearly,
even the sister he incessantly teases.
Four is an age of growing up fast;
of racing his bike or his little toy Jeep;
of energy levels no adult can outlast;
of panicking his mother with a daredevil leap.
Four is an age that comes only once
in the scheme of life's perpetual cycle;
so, we smile and we wince as we watch all his stunts,
knowing full well there's only one Michael!

July 10, 1989

Who is that racing on a two-wheel bike?
Who is that diving into the deep-water pool,
then swimming across it, unafraid and cool?
Why, it's our five-year-old grandson: it's Mighty Mike!
Who is the boy who goes off happily to camp?
Who is the boy with friends up and down the street
and the one whom mothers want their little girls to meet?
When he's dressed for a party, he's the boy who shines like a lamp.
Who is the boy who goes willingly to bed at night?
Who is the boy whose mouth is still full of thumb?
Who is the boy who commits mischief and then plays dumb?
Who is the boy—when it comes to his sister—can't resist a fight?
Who is the boy who claws like a cat?
Who is the boy who gets scolded and starts to whine,
until he senses all is clear and then murmurs, "Fine!"
His mother wants to know how you cope with a boy like that!
Well, he's only five and this is *his* bag of tricks.
We've watched another boy give his parents quite a time,
until one day they knew it was worth the tough climb.
Yet, one warning: it *won't* get better when Michael is six!

July 10, 1990

Don Mirabel

Six may be only a three-letter word,
but there are so many others we can use:
all of them, of course, we know you've heard;
so, to describe our Michael, these are the ones we choose:
He comes to mind when you say, "a real *boy*,"
with a strong desire to play to *win*;
most of the time, he's grandma's *joy*,
and a *wiz* at any game he wants to begin.
Now, *read* has four letters and so does *book*;
so does *ball* and *ride* a *bike*, too.
So, we know you'll excuse the liberty we took
in adding three words: *we love you!*

July 10, 1991

On Michael's Bar Mitzvah

According to tradition, Michael,
today you are a man.
I don't know where or why
this attitude began,
But, if you want my opinion,
my view of the truth,
you have plenty of time
to sacrifice your youth.
Let me give you this advice, grandson:
before there is a world to conquer,
there is a ball game to be won;
before you take on the serious stuff,
there is still a lot of fun.
Welcome the pleasures of growing up:
you will know when your manhood has begun!
Time, as they say, is on your side;
savor your youth as much as you can;
enjoy the freedom; enjoy the ride,
and *then* you can say, "Today, I am a man!"

July 10, 1998

Don Mirabel

EASTON & BRANDON

On Easton's Birth

O, welcome to the world, son of my son!
The journey's long and has just begun.
The road's not paved with yellow bricks, nor leads
to paradise, but it can serve your needs
if you follow your heart and pursue your goal.
Be not diverted by every bend, control
the urge to blend, be true to your higher
calling: be the idol to whom others aspire.
A perfect world, you see, it can never be,
so, waste no time on prayer or reverie.
Seek to expand the horizons of man's mind;
with someone special share the satisfaction you find.
Be kind, be caring, and let love always abound,
and the world you leave will be much better than you found.

October 14, 1998

Don Mirabel

My little man, the years are swift
and this is but the first;
through these days you have been our gift,
with a smile that sates our thirst.
To watch you grow, the things you do
(with a special, endearing flair),
the "bye-bye" wave, the "peek-a-boo,"
"How big..." with hands high in the air.
The world grows wider as you grow older;
there is much you will discover.
Snuggled on your parent's shoulder,
you learn the lesson of the lover.
So—that is what we wish today
and on every birthday after:
let love guide you along life's way,
just blend it with wisdom and laughter.

October 14, 1999

How do we describe a boy of two?
How do we make our description effective?
We must choose words that ring perfectly true;
so, we'll start with the word, "detective."
Everything is of interest to him;
his curiosity can not be defied.
Closet doors open and close at his whim,
until he has rearranged everything inside.
"Funny singing" also enters our mind;
after daddy's "Happy together" comes his booming shout;
he follows up this one very much in kind
with "Woof, woof" when he hears "Who let the dogs out?"
Another word is "lover"—that's easy to see:
there's always a kiss for mom and for dad,
but also for baby Brandon and the whole family.
He has the makings of a really fine lad.
So, on your second birthday, dear Easton, dear boy.
we, too, have some words that fit like a glove:
you're a "handful," a "delight," a "world of joy,"
you brighten our day and fill our hearts with love.

October 14, 2000

Don Mirabel

Fourteen is an enigmatic age: too young
to be grown-up, 'though Nature disagrees.
At this age the mind may run slower than the tongue;
the heart may react faster than the eye sees.
You'll make mistakes from which there's much to learn.
The possible will become a puzzling maze.
Many paths will appear; you'll wonder where to turn:
so much of growing-up is life in a daze.
Think hard to find and follow a worthy goal—
along the way the maze will surely clear.
The parts will slowly meld and become whole,
and you will sense when your success is near.
Seek only positive things to bring you joy
and you'll be on your way to outgrowing the boy.

October 14, 2012

One is a wonderful age;
like a star on a stage:
all eyes beguiled,
simply because he smiled!
Brandon means fun
as he plays with his toys,
and valiantly tries
to keep up with the boys.
Brandon means strong
as he tugs on his mother,
or, by refusing to yield,
he frustrates his brother.
Brandon means happy:
he'd rather smile than cry;
fascinated by new things
he is curious to try.
Brandon means love,
and Brandon means laughter;
may both always be with him
forever after!

February 23, 2001

Don Mirabel

MISCELLANEOUS

DON'T CALL IT 'LIFE'

There are many cities I still yearn to see.
There is much wisdom I still wish to gain.
There are a thousand things that beckon me
and yet a rush of time I can't restrain.
Must I reach the end with just a bitter taste
as I am abandoned at the future's edge?
Must I take with me only a sense of waste
as I stand trembling on life's final ledge?

O, God or Father Time or simply Age:
You tempt me with a world of wondrous things,
with love and all the pleasures I engage,
yet abide the sadness that their ending brings.
   Don't call it "life:" you're slowly killing me!
   Don't close my eyes: I won't go willingly!

April, 2011

Don Mirabel

O, Father Who hides in heaven, please answer us!
Those who speak for You are inflated by their power.
The world is frightful, ridden by hate, cancerous,
fraught with evil from which our souls cower.
Where were You during the dreadful Holocaust?
Does a Father abandon his children in a time of need?
Millions of innocent lives were tortured and lost.
You allowed the Devil to flourish and succeed!
Why did You permit the horror of 9/11?
Why claim the dead and destroy the living, as well?
Was this Your way to lure them to heaven
and condemn their loved ones to a living hell?
　　Why did You let evil and ignorance persist?
　　Father, please answer us: Do You exist?

September, 2011